Stars in the Atacama

Jelisa Jeffery

BookLeaf
Publishing

India | USA | UK

Presentation by *BookLeaf Publishing*

Web: www.bookleafpub.com

E-mail: info@bookleafpub.com

ISBN: 9789357447041

First edition 2022

DEDICATION

I dedicate this book to my lost but not forgotten friend, Danielle Handrahan.

ACKNOWLEDGEMENT

I would first like to thank nature, for being a never-ending pit of inspiration.
Secondly, my parents and step-parents for believing in me no matter where I venture or what goals I strive for. And lastly, my misfortunes, for never being something I can't handle, but always being something I can write about.

PREFACE

The following poems are written with intention and deep meaning, and are here, sandwiched between a front and back cover for your perusing (or to not peruse, if you wish). These poems are sometimes negative and sometimes positive, but I hope every one of them is to your liking (or disliking, as that can be equally memorable).

My Pottery

I'll pull out a single hair,
For every time I'm told,
"At least you're pretty",
Or how to wear my dress
Equivocal but delusional,
As appearance will always be a mere vessel.
We do not judge a vase — we see the flowers it
holds inside.
Why do our eyes deceive us,
Why do we play with coats and pony-tails
And high-heeled regrets
And tight waists — as if only for display,
And not to function as a tool of mobility.
And arriving late because you had to shave
Why do we scrutinize the vase?
I tug another hair,
For every time a person whistles at my walk
As if I prowl on cement in search of applause for
my appearance
Why do we adhere
To such an inverse morality?
We are ignominious archetypes.
Have we been created in a factory or
organically?
I'll pull these hairs out

For every time my outward self is the only thing
someone cares to know
And I'll be bald when I'm done
And they'll know the shape of my scalp
But they'll never know my abstract thought,
Or useful perspective,
Or witty humour, constructive temper
Or remember tremendous and wise things I've
said
In their un-breaking stare at my bald head
In their gaze at my vase,
Bypassing my mind,
Ignoring the woolly violet on the inside

Emerald Blanket

The sun greets me in pieces, through the
evergreens' needles and limbs,
Tickling bits of dust particles,
And air-born, fluttery spores,
Soothing my goosebumps.
But the wooded labyrinth has a magnetizing
aroma,
One of eerie descent
That I can't let go of,
Even with the subdued lullaby of warm, midday
light.
I crave the unnerving mystery
That the tall, stoic, ligneous soldiers give
without hesitation.
I want to be caught with my heart in my throat,
And my breath unattainable.
I want their twigs and wiggly things
Wriggling in my core,
And hear my heartbeat thumping: "more!"
And befall my breathy song;
My wail
That never ends,
Until I find the forest center.
Where most are lost,
I'm found.

Yet to Be

I'm a poem — but what are you?
You're a person who can see,
Or at the very least, read
With your fingers, if need be.
I'm a stringing of words
And I have a message to display.
What have you? What do you do?
What do you have to say?
And what is your name?
My name is yet to be.
I am made up of vowels,
And punctuation,
And sounds, as long as you say me out loud.
What are you made of?
A body, and feelings, and wonderful things?
Are you made of atoms and cells?
I am words on a screen,
Or in a book,
But it turns out I am more than just that.
I am an epiphany of yours,
One you haven't had yet,
But will.
One that will exist because of you;
Because of me.
Because of this poem.

You'll see.
As I am yet to be.

Stolen Home

Five fingers.
Five fingers too late, and an empty plate.

Wasted day.
Wasted fate, wasted away.

They say it's always darkest before morning,
Yet dawn is a moment that we sleep through.
We miss it,
We reel it in with fishing rods,
We wish it near,
We kiss it when it's here.

But we are usually too busy to see it,
Our beady eyes focused on reliving the past.

Misery will attach like a leech.
And regret is a creep
Who lurks in the woods behind maple leaves.

Above closed eyelids
Does hope make a home.

Overcoming what's been done
Is not a race of hare and tortoise,

It's the bullet of a gun.

I am a foreign song,
Resident of a place I don't belong.

Reptile Shell

Painted plastic, the brushes stroke,
Camouflaged as diamond stone.
Beneath the cloak of white-blue sky,
The granite cries alone.

Above the puddle, although wee
His belly masked in lily pad.
The pond beside, he takes a peek,
While wishing he was grand.

Poking out of tortoise attire,
The bird beak pecks the grounded corn.
Though the other winged prey higher,
She yearned to be earth-bourn.

If we fill the water of wishing wells,
If we gladly call the puddle a pond,
We break biologic boundary spells
And sing our fateful songs.

Chanticleer

Caricature of a truth.
I lay down my wheat and fire iron.
In smoky mirrors, I spread my tail feathers
Alongside the peacock.

When will time be fated to wrist restraints;
When will the Milky Way dance?

If we pick the leaves of the blueberry bush,
Should we ask how she feels of it?
I will dress her in new garb
Before the rooster crows,
If she so wishes.

Why must we play riddles with the unknown?
We poke fun at the things we should practice.
We don't know the invisible barricade
Unless we paint it.
If we paint it.
Will we paint it?

And when eyes fall,
Of royal silk red,
And swords collide,
Will all be sought?

Have we learned already as Homo sapiens?
Have we forgotten?

Sharpened knife,
And quarterstaff.
The dermis artist before you,
Decorticating all who disobey.
All who fall astray,
Or choose a better tree to climb.
How do we not see?
How do we not see that we are blind?

And when will we learn?
When will we be taught what is wrong?
Will we ever know,
Will we ever know of what is true and sure?
Will we ever know,
What is wrong?

The rooster crows
The rooster's song.
The rooster knows.
The rooster knows.

Of Ghosts

If a voice
Flutters through walls,
Or seeps from my pillow —
If a voice calls,
I want to know their name.

A wandering soul who once lived
With body and skin,
As I,
So why should I cry at the sight?
And why is darkness
What we see,
In the souls of the dead?
I see light.

Villainous hands
Belong to the living.
The dead have redeemed.
Lost souls, unattached
To bodily wrong.

The soul:
The epitome of glorious, ignorant life —
Unbiased, unbound.
Clean,

Refreshing breeze,
That raise hairs on my skin,
But I don't run away.

Come sit,
Or dance with the sun-sparkled dust.
Peruse through the books
On bowed shelf.
Come sing of borrowed voices.
Come dine.
And exist in a place
Without exile.

If a spirit is searching
For a home between lives,
A place to rest —
Like the bird makes a nest,
Let it be.
I don't weep,
I make friends
With the ghost that lives with me.
I am shell
To the slug you call ugly.

I am haunted.
Don't worry for me.

I am haunted,
But I want to be.

Lessons From the Dire Wolf

Don't ask why all must end —
Without end,
There would not be beginning.

There would not be reason,
Or lesson,
Or strength.

Without death,
No life.
No wonder,
No loss.

Toxins would fester beneath skin,
And without ending,
Your patience wears thin,
If nothing ends,
We give in.
Nobody wins.

Without closure,

Without moving on,
Without change:
Doors stay closed,
All is mediocre,
And bland to the taste.
Nothing improves.
Everything stays.

Don't ask why all must end.
We know pain like a close friend,
When the end visits,
And it costs us large sums
Of ourselves.
But beginnings are not born
Without help.
New life doesn't sprout —
The fungus doesn't grow
Without the fallen green turning grey.

Don't ask why.
It ends because it must.
Trust the stops the train takes on the way.
Grieve,
And cry until sober of sorrow,
But know,
That today's end
Brings tomorrow.

To Whom it May Matter...

The fact of the matter,
That matters,
Is that you matter,
No matter what matters to others.
We're sisters and brothers,
We're all made of matter.
You don't matter less,
No matter your dress.
And no matter our differences.
He or her,
Or they, for that matter,
You matter the same.
No matter your looks,
No matter the thinner or fatter,
And no matter your name,
You matter.

Elspeth Reoch

My magick incantation
Is never faded or outdated.
When the earth knows deterioration
I feel a responsibility, a reaction,
A habit forming,
A sorcery alluring.
I feel a voice, concerning, calling.
I'll conjure my knowledge,
Nestled safely on broomstick,
And take hitch,
Pitch my best, paint the peeling patches,
Seek solutions to problems,
And pour the answers in the cauldron.
The ways to heal the earth are finding me.
My voice reverberates
Through spoken spells.
I can yell!
I can tell the stories,
While my sisters lived mute,
And knew the inside of a casket too early.
Too often misunderstood,
Punished for what they cast.
And simply because of
The timing of my birth,
I'm worth more than my kin,

Of years before.
I won't be hung for writing this,
I won't have to prepare my lips
For death's kiss,
Even if I was a witch.

Incantations

I.
Bare-footed frolic,
In forest of peril,
To dine with the swine,
Though filthy and feral,
We eat with the pig,
We feast on the wheat,
We banish the wolf,
Who we don't wish to meet.

II.
Below, befallen brothers,
Laying vertical in oak,
Defend my earthly body
Cover me in cloak.

Souls of loved departed,
Who whistle in the trees,
Redirect the cacodemon
The one who waits for me.

Spirit of the past,
Soothe with healing chants
Be my blinded eyes,
Protect me when I can't.

III.
Bewitching
Betwixt the realm
Betwixt the elm and willow
Climb the hill
Of counting sheep
In search of sleep
Along your pillow.
Let eyes grow weary more;
Let dreams,
Let nightly scenes redeem,
And let soar
The fairy who flies
In search of eyes, wide awake.
Let me find
The lullaby,
To lull to rest
Until the next daybreak.

IV.
Which one will help me there?
The owl or the fox?
The leaping frog beyond the marsh,
The eagle or the hawk?
Who will be my spotting eye?
The "X" that marks my way?
I need the spirit's guiding light
To not be led astray.

V.
Fire, red
And fire, high,
Beyond the line,
Beyond the sky
Ball of light,
Sphere of gas
Bless my soul
And cleanse my past.

Nightly phase,
Nightly scene,
Moon of magic
Time of dreams,
Wish me well,
Come to play,
Guide my footing,
Guide my way.

Thoughts Before Death

You find yourself in the deep dark beneath,
And you find a key.
Unlocking years of answers
And redeeming reasons for misery lived.

Why?

With crusty eyes and dark, damp lips,
Do you find the list now?

Why do you find it buried amongst maggots
And phyllophaga larvae,
When it sails in large, beautiful ships on the sea,
And falls with the rain,
And places recognizable prints
Alongside our own.
Dusty traces on door knobs
And window sills.

Can you find what makes you whole
Before your final breath?
It whispers in your ears by the willow.

And it seeps into cobblestone cracks.
Why can we never find what's next,
Until we're beneath it?

Birthday Party

I looked at the circle
And it was a square.

Friendly emotions
Are divisible by small numbers,
But crowds give me a bad taste.

I click the metal counter,
I'm at 26 questions starting with "why",
And my memory
Is a dish of expired food in the fridge.

A figure of many
Futures
Stands at my front door,
But I don't answer
To unexpected guests,
And my mailbox is a
Pocket of regret.

My attempts like dirt on buckskin,
But the moon
And sun
Both know the time I put in.

If only they could speak for me.

When the life inside my head
Infiltrates the life that others see,
I am the servant to emotion.
I am the sleeping circus lion behind iron.

When others see the best in me,
It's unrequited.
How can we reside in a place we're uninvited?
And we pretend we like to fight
For the issues we birth.
The hearse we take turns driving to the cliff,
To kill it again.

Feed your inner child
Feed the flame
And tame the opposing winds,
As a child knows,
Their mind, unbiased
And blind to the color of skin.

We learn the bad things
Like we learn to crack a coconut,
To eat the fruit within.
We think it is a victory.

Remember me in dried flowers
And genmaicha tea,

Or not at all.

If you must,
Feed the jowls,
But let the child win.

Stars in the Atacama

The corn maze is my mind;
A fetal idea; the resonance of the project,
untouched.
The haunting song of the unexplored map,
The call of the camel's back.
Feet planted in deep, rooted dirt,
If only in water, I'd swim;
If only in air, I'd fly.

The corrosion;
Focus fades and motivation moves on
And I fear the exposure of attempts untaken,
As my odyssey calls like a red-tailed hawk.
I stay like a sunflower,
Facing the right way, but stationary.
I'll stare eyes with evocative valleys,
And run river rapids in my mind,
But I'll remain in sinking sand.
Though heavenly celestial views lie overhead,
I'm hindered still,
Until I walk out of the desert.

The Red Faced Boat

She longs for the boat with the red face.
The red faced boat
In the big blue sea,
By the lighthouse peak
On the shore.

She calls, like a foghorn, to the sky.
A foghorn call,
In the thick of cloud,
By the lighthouse peak
On the shore.

She wails for the others lost beneath.
Songs for the lost
To the crashing wave,
By the lighthouse peak
On the shore.

She haunts below like a thalassic ghost.
Her haunting past,
When her boat capsized,
By the lighthouse peak
On the shore.

Circus Act

Hush, now.
A blistered retort;
You shadow your existence and intentions.
I see through your timeless quilt
That you stitched with charlatan hands.
All the world lays eyes on your gnarled face.
The clock takes lives,
And fate takes a cigarette break.
Nonetheless, I find you frozen.
You don't run from the katzenjammer jester,
You hide.
You don't admit your illicit deeds,
You hold the wooden cross of the marionette.
No matter how forcibly your thread pulls,
The lion won't feed on the dangled meat.
Your puppet drowns alone;
No one cheers for the enemy.

Salina

The tree sobs happily,
In milky water.
The water bug kisses the fetid foliage.
And all is damp.
All is good.

The marsh is alive in the night.
The call of the cricket leg plays,
Along to the baritone frog croak.
All is good in the marsh.

Muted tones of green
And copper
Grow short and tall,
Sprouting from their liquid home.
Grey stones
(But you wouldn't know),
Carpeted in moss and lichen.

So dead,
So alive.
The mystery,
As sweet as the cool lacquer of dew
Misting over me.
I blink the haze from my eyes.

Aye,
But I still cry.
I still weep with delight,
Of the sight before me.
I cry with the tree.

And by sun,
The milk-water looks as ice,
That moves as gelatinous dancers,
Or as silk
In the wind.

If the rain only knew,
That the swamp will be wet either way.
But when the sky
Matches color and dress
With the grungy mire,
Everything looks as it should.
All is good.

Without Forced Hand

Vineyard of vermilion.
A bind holding hands in entranced sky,
While the bird lays beneath,
And the pig flies.

The labyrinthine stone,
The intricate, desired key.
We mourn the bloody flesh
Between crooked teeth.

I'm cold in my blanket.
The diamond pen writing ugly names,
While we encourage
The very same.

We pick-pocket the honey of bees,
And sinking eyes notice more
Than the spyglass.
We ask the wrong questions.
Fire knows a place beneath my skin,
My heart of fertile earth,
Unscathed by the cult or the creed.

Vigour of the bully,
The scar of the fossilized abuse,
While bodies dangle
Of the mangled noose.

Graveyard pursuit;
We dig the bones of yesteryear,
But we don't clean off the dirt,
Or wipe the tear.

Beyond the known sky,
Truth lives in a lonely house.
When the lunch bell rings,
The lion is food for the mouse.

We pick-pocket the honey of bees,
Unscathed by the cult or the creed.

World Peace

Wood upon wood,
I build the wall a door.
The wall that stood tall between foe,
And now stands,
As proof that held hands
Can come without gloves
And wounds.

Cheek upon cheek,
I spread the water leaked
Of eyes once grown sore and red,
To water the bountiful garden,
That community gathered
To sow,
In unsalted field.

We may still have foe.
There are those
Who comb the horse's mane,
And those who steal the tail.

But upon your knock at our door,
We don't paint the mask of your past
Across your face.
We embrace tomorrow's peace.

Why do we fight
Over cocoa and ivory?
Our birth is not a contract
To pick a side.
Yet we still erect a divide.

Light upon dark.
As mountains crumble,
As mountains grow,
We can change as friends, from foe.

Fear

"Fear is a place",
I told the hissing shadow.
"You can't choose if you end up there, but once
there, you can choose whether or not you want
to stay".

Fear was baffled,
And bellowed, suddenly, like a bronze cannon,
"I'm real just like you! How can I be a place if
I'm standing right here".

"Because a real person still exists if you walk
away."

Ironic Thank-You Note

Can I be the man in the woods?
Who walks with viridescent leaves,
And reaches like branches
With purpose?

Can I be him —
He who couldn't be bothered
Whether empty sea-salt shells
Lie against his stalk?
His talented, contorted arms
Pimpled in thin, brittle bird eggs.
Home to the silk-giving wolf spider.

He knows vines,
Not as something that strangulates,
But as garment.
Saprophyte and toadstool
Like jewelry,
Dress his textured body.
Extravagant, speckled robe for his promotion,
Into new life-giving.

And if I can't be him,
Can I at least ask what it is
To know the sky closely?
And how it feels
To speak so clearly without voice?
To root-dance —
To be the rooftop of the rabbit,
And the watchtower for the owl.
To taste earth-given water with taproot,
And stand as a landmark
For the soaring hawk.
I know he would tell me,
He loves to share.

His nurturing stance.
He smiles at the small aphid who feeds.
And without needing anything in return,
He gives riches to the forest,
Endlessly,
Even long after he falls.
Aye, like a Phoenix,
He may even be born again
Of his own remains.

I wish I could be him.
But instead,
I write these wishes
Upon his pulpy skin.

www.ingramcontent.com/pod-product-compliance
Lightning Source LLC
La Vergne TN
LVHW041244200726
843507LV00013B/2810